KIDS' COLORING BOOK

TAME your THOUGHT MONSTER

A COLOR, LEARN, AND FEEL-GOOD BOOK FOR KIDS

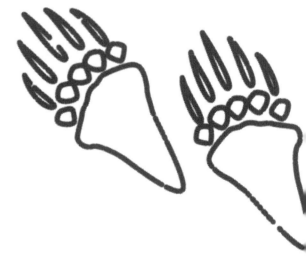

BY KATIE MCCLAIN
Katie McClain Ma Vie Magique
McClain Consulting Services, Inc.

DRAWINGS BY
Matthew McClain

ADDITIONAL DRAWINGS BY
Chuck McClain
Katie McClain

COVER AND BOOK DESIGN BY
Drai Bearwomyn

EDITED BY
Grace Kerina

FIRST EDITION
ISBN-13: 978-1483941066
ISBN-10: 148394106X
Printed in the USA

LEARN MORE AND CONTACT KATIE
www.katiemcclain.com
katie@katiemcclain.com

for

my

family

WITH
LOVE

TABLE OF CONTENTS

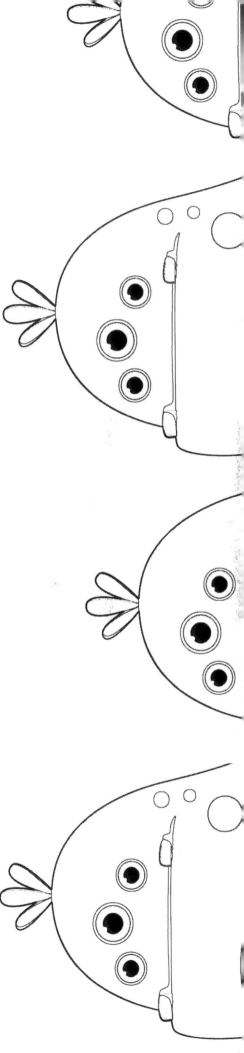

WELCOME

I'm so excited you have this book.

I created this coloring book to help you learn about your thinking and to help you feel better. After you meet your Thought Monster you can get better grades, worry less, have more fun, and be happier.

I want you to know that Thought Monsters are not supposed to be scary. A Thought Monster is kind of like a mischievous imaginary friend. Kids and grown-ups both have these imaginary friends called Thought Monsters. But, guess what? Sometimes Thought Monsters are not very helpful. Thought Monsters can keep us feeling stuck. Your Thought Monster might try to convince you not to try new things that could help you learn and have more fun.

Have you ever really wanted to try something new, but were a little bit afraid? Perhaps you were afraid to learn to swim or to ride your bike. Perhaps you were really nervous on the first day of school.

It's natural to be a little bit nervous about new things, but Thought Monsters don't like new things AT ALL. So when you want to try something new, your Thought Monster will whisper thoughts to you that might make you feel so afraid that you don't ever even try.

A bit later in the book, you'll get to meet your Thought Monster, but first you'll meet Charlie the Robot, who will help you learn to be a robot and look at just the facts about the things that happen in your life. Next, you'll learn all about feelings and how to use the Find-Your-Feeling Ladder. Then Action Annie will show you how to be a super hero by using your very own powerful thoughts. In the end, if you try out all the tools, you'll see that you've become the magician in your own life.

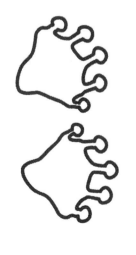

FIVE TOOLS FOR TELLING BETTER STORIES

Do you think happy stories are best? I do. I think stories with happy endings are the most fun, and they feel great.

This coloring book shows you how to tell true stories about your life that make you feel good. It's possible to make any story feel happier. Even a sad story can make you feel happy – you just need to look for the true parts of the story that feel good. Sometimes a story can make you feel happy because you learned something new from your experience.

There are five special tools that can help you tell better stories about your life:

1. **CHARLIE THE ROBOT** – **Circumstances** are the everyday facts of the things that happen each day. Charlie the Robot helps you look at just the facts of things that happen in your day. Circumstances can make us think thoughts.

2. **YOUR THOUGHT MONSTER** – **Thoughts** are what make up the stories we tell about our day. Meet your Thought Monster and spy on the thoughts it sends you. We can choose to think thoughts that make us feel good or bad.

3. **THE FIND-YOUR-FEELING LADDER** – **Feelings** are vibrations we feel in our bodies. The Find-Your-Feeling Ladder helps us name our feelings. When we think thoughts about circumstances, it causes us to feel feelings.

4. **ACTION ANNIE** – **Actions** are something we do or don't do, depending on how we feel. Good feelings help us to take helpful action, bad feelings help us to take actions that are not helpful. Action Annie will help you be a Super Hero with your actions.

5. **THE MAGICIAN** – **Results** come from the actions we take. You are the Magician in your own life when you use thoughts to improve your results in life. We get results from the actions we take.

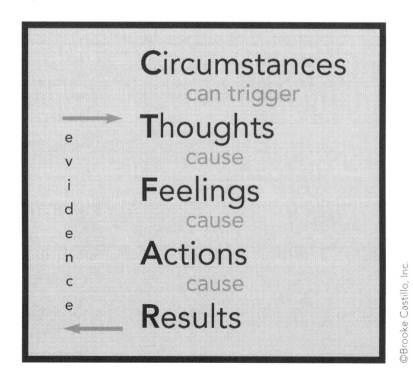

To show you how the five tools work, I'll tell you a story. The story is about a brother and sister who were playing video games. The brother got mad at the sister because he thought she was being unfair and not letting him win, so the brother quit playing games with his sister and was unhappy.

1   CHARLIE THE ROBOT helps us see just the facts of the **Circumstances**:

Circumstance: Brother & sister playing video games.

2   Spying on our **YOUR THOUGHT MONSTER** shows us feel-bad **Thoughts**:

Thought: My sister never lets me win.

3   THE FIND-YOUR-FEELING LADDER helps us name the **Feelings**:

Feeling: Mad.

4.   ACTION ANNIE helps us recognize helpful and unhelpful **Actions**:

Action: Yell at sister. Stop playing video games with sister.

5.   All the tools help you be a **MAGICIAN** in your life to create better **Results**:

Result: Not improving at playing videos, unhappy, fighting.

This is an unhappy story because brother's Thought Monster sent him the feel-bad thought about his sister not letting him win. Since the brother didn't know ANYTHING about Thought Monsters, he believed the feel-bad thought about his sister not letting him win was true. The brother felt mad and yelled at his sister and stopped playing video games with her. The brother ended up in a fight with his sister, he stopped playing games, he was unhappy, and he didn't improve his video game skills. All because of one feel-bad thought that his Thought Monster sent him!

The five tools in this book can help you understand how the stories you tell yourself with your thoughts can make you feel bed. When we tell feel-bad stories, we take action that doesn't help us and we get stuck.

Understanding how your thoughts make you feel can help you create true stories that feel good and that are helpful to you.

Let's get started coloring and learning!

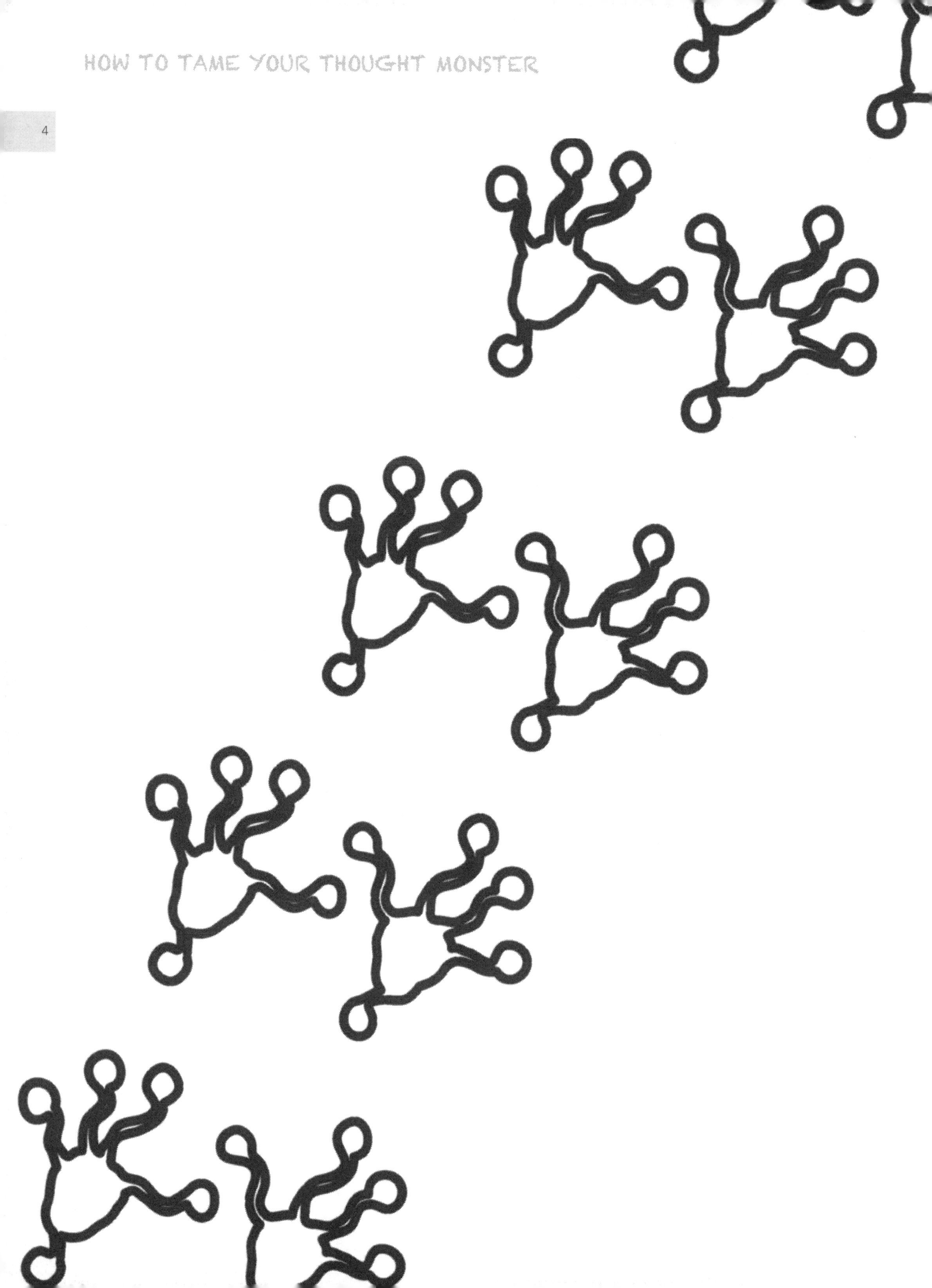

CIRCUMSTANCES

PART ONE

"Think left and think right
and think low and
think high. Oh, the
THINKS you can think
up if only you try!"

Dr. Seuss

Circumstances are the things that happen in our lives. Here are some examples of Circumstances:

- Wake up from sleeping.
- Go to school.
- Do homework.
- Play with friends.
- Take a test.

Do you know any robots that feel emotions? I don't. Charlie the Robot can help you **find the facts** of the things that happen in your life. Robots don't feel emotions or feelings. Robots **only observe the facts** of the things that happen.

Circumstances don't have any feelings or emotions attached to them. If we observe **exactly what happened**, we won't feel happy or sad. We'll just see facts without feel-bad or feel-good emotions.

Pretend to be a robot like Charlie and look at the things that happened in your day today. When you're pretending to be a robot, try to **only see the facts** of what happened. Take out all the feel-bad emotions of what happened.

Here's a story. See if you can **Find the Facts**:

Susie and Tracy were playing together. Tracy chose to be the leader. That meant Susie was the follower. Susie didn't want to be the follower. Susie cried and told her mom that Tracy was bossy!

Here are some of the facts you (and Charlie the Robot) might have discovered:

Susie and Tracey talked and played.
Tracy chose to be the leader.
Tears came out of Susie's eyes.
Susie said words to her mom.

You don't need to pretend to be a robot and look at the facts if you feel good or happy about something that happened. Pretend to be a robot and find the facts when something happens that makes you feel bad, sad, or scared.

On the next page, try the exercise with Charlie the Robot to help you **Find the Facts** of things that happened.

8

EXERCISE
FOR THE ADULTS | FIND THE FACTS

Think about what happened today. Find the Facts about some of the things that happened at home, at school, with your family, and with friends. Write the Facts on the lines below as if Charlie the Robot had watched your entire day. Make sure there are no feelings or emotions when you make your list. Ask an adult for help if you need it.

I'll ask you some things to help you think about your day:

- Tell me about your friends.
- What happened at school today?
- What do you wish you could change about today?
- What's going on in your life?
- Tell me about your family.

FACT _____

FACT _____

FACT _____

FACT _____

FACT _____

FACT _____

FACT _____

FACT _____

FACT _____

FACT _____

FACT _____

FACT _____

FACT --

FACT --

FACT --

FACT --

FACT --

FACT --

FACT --

FACT --

FACT --

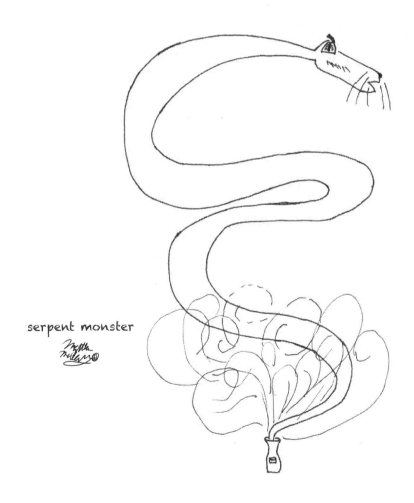

serpent monster

CIRCUMSTANCES

THINGS TO REMEMBER ABOUT CIRCUMSTANCES

- Circumstances can't be changed – especially the ones that have already happened.

- Circumstances are facts that can be proven.

- Facts don't hurt.

- Circumstances don't have to hurt our feelings.

- When we add a feeling word to a circumstance, it changes to a thought (T) that cannot be proven as fact.

Here's an example:

This is a circumstance (C):

> C I have a teacher.

This is a circumstance with a feeling word added to it:

> T I have a *mean* teacher.

- Our thoughts about our circumstances and the things that happen to us can make us feel bad or good. We can choose to feel good about our circumstances.

HELPFUL HINTS

- Ask questions to help yourself find the facts of what happened.
- Things that happened in the past are always a Circumstance.
- The words should and shouldn't never belong with the facts.

TELL A BETTER STORY

When something happens that makes you feel bad, you can use the steps below to practice telling a better story that's true and that feels good.

1   Tell the original story of what happened. Include all the feelings.

2   Be like Charlie the Robot and look for the facts.

3   Describe the details of what actually happened.

4   Take out any words that are emotional or contain judgment.

5   Tell the story again, with **just the facts** this time.

6   Re-tell your story in a way that's true and also feels good
    or makes you feel powerful.

THOUGHT'S

PART TWO

14

"A person who has good thoughts
cannot ever be ugly. You can have
a wonky nose and a crooked mouth
and a double chin and stick-out teeth,
but if you have good thoughts they
will shine out of your face like
sunbeams and you will
always look lovely."

Roald Dahl

We each have a little voice inside that sends us thoughts. Sometimes the thoughts feel bad and we get stuck or scared and we stop trying. That voice is called a **Thought Monster.** When we meet our Thought Monster, we can start to notice and ignore the feel-bad thoughts it sends us and choose to think feel-good thoughts instead.

Your Thought Monster is the voice inside that discourages you from trying new things. It tells you when it thinks you did a bad job or didn't work hard. Your Thought Monster sometimes says that you aren't as smart or as fast or pretty as another person. Thought Monsters can stop us from reaching our goals.

Your Thought Monster doesn't want you to change, because that would be scary for your Monster. Your Thought Monster thinks it is helping you when it whispers thoughts like these to you:

- You are not smart enough.
- They won't like you.
- You messed that up.
- You can't do this.

Each of us has a unique Thought Monster. Though Monsters are different, just like people are all different. Some Thought Monsters are boys, some are girls, and some are just things.

This is Ronaldo. He's my son's Thought Monster. I think he's cute. There's no need to be afraid of or mad at our Thought Monsters. Even though our Thought Monsters are just trying to help us, most of the thoughts our Thought Monsters send make us feel bad.

On the next page, you'll get to meet your Thought Monster. Then find the feel-bad thoughts your Monster sends you. Don't believe those feel-bad thoughts! They're not true or helpful.

ronaldo

HERE ARE MORE THOUGHT MONSTERS

spitebird

MEET YOUR THOUGHT MONSTER

Have you heard the crummy thoughts your Monster sends you? Do you know what your Monster looks like? Does it have a name?

Meeting your Thought Monster is an easy way to notice your feel-bad thoughts so you can change to them into feel-good thoughts.

On the next page, draw your Thought Monster. Here's how:

1   **Take a couple of deep breaths and get quiet for a minute.**

2   **Close your eyes and listen for your Thought Monster.**

3   **Now draw it.**

- Is it wearing anything?
- Does it have a particular job?
- Does it use tools or props?

4   **Listen for your Thought Monster's name.**

5   **Spy on your Thought Monster to discover the feel-bad thoughts it tries to send you.**

When you start noticing the feel-bad thoughts, ask these questions about the thoughts you hear:

- How do I feel when I think this thought?
- How big is this thought? Can I make it smaller?
- Can I find anything funny about this thought?
- If my mom or dad was thinking this thought, what would I say to help them feel better?
- Can I throw this thought away?

Practice letting go of feel-bad thoughts. Practice switching to thoughts that feel better when you think them.

You can make your Thought Monster into a puppet! Ask your parents for permission to find out how to make one by going to this page online:

http://katiemcclain.com/tametmresources/thoughtmonsterpuppet/

Have fun discovering your Thought Monster!

18

FOR THE ADULTS | DRAW YOUR THOUGHT MONSTER

Use your favorite markers or crayons and draw the Thought Monster that you saw in your imagination. Don't be scared! Your Thought Monster wants to help you, even though it doesn't do a very good job.

Be a spy and listen to your Thought Monster. What do you hear your Thought Monster say to you that makes you feel bad?

What feel-good thought can you think and believe about yourself instead of listening to your Thought Monster?

THOUGHTS

THINGS TO REMEMBER ABOUT THOUGHTS

▓ We think thoughts about our Circumstances.

▓ Spy on your Thought Monster so you can find and change feel-bad thoughts.

▓ Thoughts that feel bad are not necessarily true.

▓ Thoughts that feel good and make you feel strong are thoughts that are true for you.

▓ The more feel-good thoughts that you think, the more feel-good feelings and creations you will have in your life.

▓ Try to take the feeling words out of a thought. If the new thought is true and it feels better, you created a feel-good thought!

HELPFUL HINTS

Try using these thoughts as new, feel-better thoughts:

T I can do this.
T I'm learning all the time.
T I can choose feel-good thoughts.
T I'm smart.
T I'm happy.
T I love me.
T I belong here.
T I can be myself.
T I'm good enough.
T He/she is doing their best.
T I create my life.

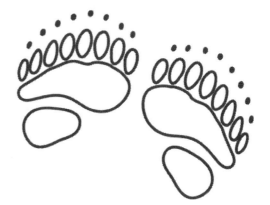
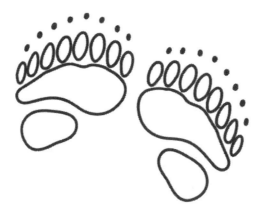
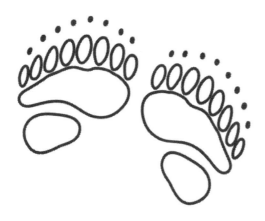
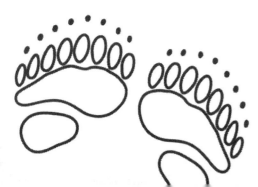

FEELINGS

PART THREE

"Whatever you do,
you should do it with feeling."

Yogi Berra

USING THE FIND-YOUR-FEELING LADDER

Use this Find-Your-Feeling Ladder to help you name your feelings. The circle in the middle of the Ladder is called **neutral**. A neutral feeling is a feeling that's neither good nor bad. Above the circle are feel-good feelings, labeled as **Happy/Powerful Feelings**. Below the circle are feel-bad feelings, labeled as **Sad/Weak Feelings**. If you notice that you have a feel-bad feeling, you can change your thought so that you move your feelings **UP** the ladder to a better feeling. You can move up the ladder slowly or make a big jump. The most important thing to remember is that when you find a new feel-better thought, you must believe it or it won't help you.

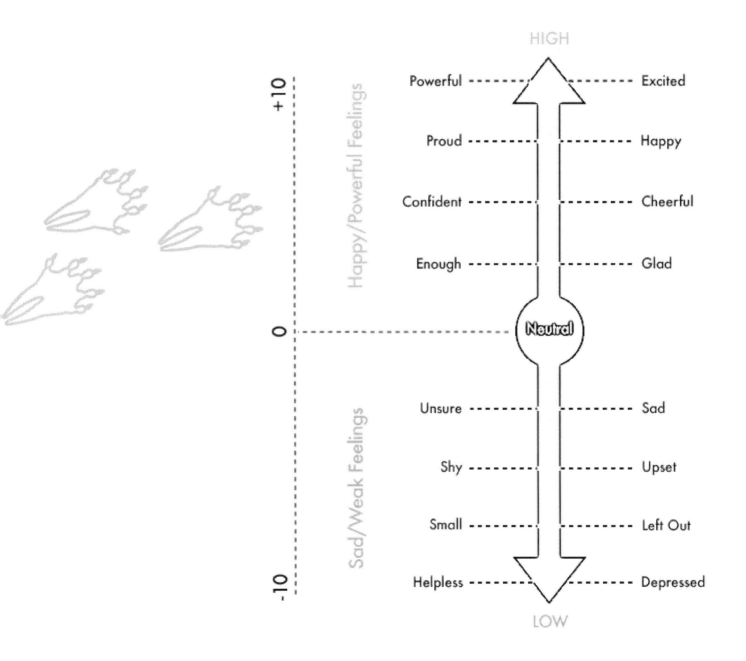

EXERCISE | DRAW YOUR FEELING

I bet you're really good at feeling your feelings. When you're happy, you smile and laugh. When you're sad, you frown and cry. Feeling your feelings is a good thing, but sometimes feelings can be scary to feel. If your feelings are too scary or too sad or too anything, please ask an adult to help you.

Think about something that makes you feel happy. Can you find that happy feeling in your body?

Describe one of your feelings and draw it out the way you did with your Thought Monster. Follow the steps below to draw how you feel right now or think of something that makes you feel happy and draw that feeling. You can draw in the blank space below.

1   First, close your eyes.

2   Pay attention to the top of your head and slowly scan your whole body.

3   Stop at different places in your body to see if you notice a feeling there.

4   Did you find a feeling?

5   Where is it?

6   Is the feeling hard or soft?

7   Is the feeling cold or hot?

8   Is the feeling fluffy or pointy?

9   Does the feeling have a color?

10   Does the feeling move or change?

11   After you've found a feeling, draw it in the space below.

12   Name the feeling with a feeling-word, like happy, sad, worried, excited, or something else. If you need help, you can check the Find-Your-Feeling Ladder on the previous page or ask an adult.

If the feeling isn't too sad or scary, watch the feeling to see if it changes. With many feelings, if you watch them they will eventually disappear.

FEELINGS
OVERVIEW & TIPS

THINGS TO REMEMBER ABOUT FEELINGS

- Emotions and feelings are vibrations in the body.

- All feelings are caused by thoughts (except feelings that happen when the weather makes us cold or hot, or when we 're sick, injured, or hungry).

- If you feel bad in some way (and you're not sick or hurt), you're probably thinking a thought that's causing the bad feeling.

- You can change how you feel by changing your thoughts.

- Practice thinking a thought and then finding the feeling in your body that's caused by that thought.

- When you allow your feelings, they quickly disappear. When you resist your feelings, they get stronger and bigger.

HOW DO YOU WANT TO FEEL?

Think about how you want to feel and then find a thought that makes you feel that way. Make sure that the new thought is true and that you believe it.

If I want to feel **happy,** I can think **of my favorite friend**!

Now you try it:

If I want to feel _____, I can think _____.

If I want to feel _____, I can think _____.

If I want to feel _____, I can think _____.

ACTIONS

PART FOUR

"Nurture your mind with great thoughts,
to believe in the heroic makes heroes."

Benjamin Disraeli

CLAIM YOUR SUPER POWER!

Do you know that you have super powers? Your super powers are the things that you do really well and that are easy for you to do. You can spend hours and hours taking action with your super powers and you barely even get tired.

Close your eyes and think about one thing you're good at. It could be drawing, playing sports, reading, dancing, or something else.

Action Annie's main super power is noticing her thoughts. Annie's super power is called **self-awareness**. Annie can figure out which thoughts make her feel good and powerful, and which thoughts feel bad and aren't helpful to her. She uses her super power of self-awareness to choose thoughts that feel good so she can take powerful actions. Annie thinks her most powerful thoughts over and over to become a super hero in her own life.

The more you notice your thoughts and find the thoughts that make you feel good, like Action Annie does, the more of a hero you can be in your own life.

Annie is super aware of her thoughts. She notices the way her thoughts make her feel, and she chooses powerful thoughts that support her actions. Be a super hero in your own life by becoming super aware of your thoughts, too!

EXERCISE | DRAW YOUR SUPER POWER

Think about something you do that you're really good at. That's a super power. What do you think or tell yourself right before you use that super power?

Draw a picture of yourself using your super power.

Write the thoughts you think when you're using your super power.

THINGS TO REMEMBER ABOUT ACTIONS

- Actions are all the things you **do**.

- Actions are powered by your feelings, and your feelings come from your thoughts.

- If you want to change your actions, first change your thoughts.

- To take the actions you want to take, apply the same feel-good thinking that helps you when you do actions you're already good at.

- Think about someone you know who takes actions that you want to take. Try out the thoughts you imagine they think. See if those thoughts help you take the action you want to take.

HOW TO CHANGE YOUR ACTIONS

Do you have any habits or behaviors you want to change? The questions below can help you change an action you don't want into a more powerful action:

- What action do you want to take?

- What feeling would give you the power to take that action?

- What thought could you think to help you feel the feeling that will power the action you want to take?

Or try this:

- Think of someone you like who does the powerful action you want to do.

- What do you imagine that person **thinks** before they take the action?

- Try the same thought for yourself to see if it powers your feelings to take the action you want.

RESULTS

PART FIVE

"There is no such thing as failure.
There are only results."

Tony Robbins

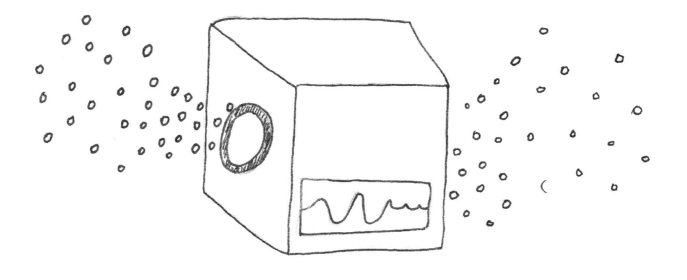

cube monster

If you've tried all the tools in this book, congratulations! You're practicing being a Magician in your own life.

Here's a top hat and a magic wand to make your magic more official:

The Magician (you!) knows how to use thoughts, feelings, and actions to create results that are wanted and that feel good.

This book has shown you the magic formula for getting results that you like:

- Get to know your Thought Monster. Spy on your Thought Monster anytime to notice any feel-bad thoughts it's sending you. Then you can choose to change them to feel-good thoughts.

- Practice describing and drawing your feelings. When you practice staying with feelings that aren't too scary, you can often watch them disappear like magic.

- Pay attention to your feel-good thoughts. You can choose to think feel-good thoughts that power you to take super-hero actions.

Good job being a Magician!

As the Magician of your life, keep practicing the tools in this book to help you create as much happiness and fun as you want.

RESULTS

OVERVIEW & TIPS

THINGS TO REMEMBER ABOUT RESULTS AND BEING A MAGICIAN IN YOUR LIFE

- A result is something you create with your thoughts.

- If you want to do better in your life, think better thoughts so you can feel better and act more powerfully.

- If you want to get better grades, improve in sports, have fun friendships, and be happier, find better-feeling thoughts that help you take better actions.

SEE HOW AWESOME YOU ARE!

- What are some things about yourself that you're proud of?

- Why are you proud of those things about yourself?

- What are some of the feel-good thoughts you think which make you feel proud?

- Keep thinking feel-good thoughts!

HOW TO IMPROVE THE RESULTS IN YOUR LIFE

1 Make a list of some areas in your life you want to improve, like sibling relationships, friendships, grades, sports, etc.

2 How will you **feel** when you get the results you want?

3 What thought can you think **right now** to feel the feeling you'll have when you get the result you want?

4 If you think the thought that makes you feel better now, you're more likely to take the actions you need to take to improve your life.

Made in the USA
San Bernardino, CA
21 February 2019